ORDER BLOCK ORDER FLOW PROFIT KIT

THE COMPLETE MARKET MAKERS TRADING GUIDE

PROFIT   *KING*

Order blocks can be found in any market, including stocks, futures, forex, and cryptocurrencies, and they can be used in any timeframe, from minutes to weeks. Order block trading can be used in conjunction with other technical analysis tools, such as trend lines, moving averages, and oscillators, to confirm trades or spot potential trade setups.

The order block trading method involves the following standard steps.

1. Find a price chart that clearly displays areas of buying or selling activity, usually represented by a series of candles.

2. Find the most important "order blocks," also known as areas of concentrated buying or selling activity.

3. Find out if the price is likely to abide by or surpass the order block. To do this, observe the nearby price movement.

4. If the price is expected to stay within the block, think about placing a stop loss order just below or just above the block and entering a long or short trade close to the block.

Here is an illustration of a nifty 50.

This chart was taken during the day. In this case, I combined the order block and avwap indicator. Price reach confluence of order block and VWAP ZONE

NOW VERIFY THE CHART BELOW. That day, the price changed from green to red and began to decline from the tested order block zone.

Smart Money Trading Method's Fundamental Principle.

There are three parts to this concept .

Smart MONEY CONCEPT.

1. Order Block

2. Demand and Supply .

MARKET STRUCTURE SMART MONEY .

1. Break of structure

2. SD Flip

3. CHoCH

SMART MONEY ENTRY METHOD.

1. Inducement.

2. Liquidity Hunt

Order Block In Trading what Is IT?

When the market makes an impulsive move, order blocks are the tracks left behind. The Order Block (OB) is the final opposite candle before a significant move that upsets the market's equilibrium. Price is most likely to come back to those zones before it triggers another impulse move to continue his trend.

What is order block?

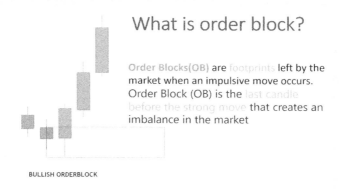

Order Blocks(OB) are footprints left by the market when an impulsive move occurs. Order Block (OB) is the last candle before the strong move that creates an imbalance in the market

BULLISH ORDERBLOCK

BEARISH ORBLOCK FORMED

REVERSAL FROM OB ZONE

Why Do We have Order Block Zone in Our Chart?

- The market kept falling after the bearish order block zone appeared, which indicates that the smart money was placing sell orders at the time it appeared (in contrast to the bullish order block zone).

- Aggressive individuals are impatient to buy or sell. To put it another way, you place a MARKET ORDER to buy or sell anything right now at the best price that is being offered.

- Because it is so big, your post won't be filled entirely at once. As the price rises quickly, the position will be divided, but it will quickly fill and you will be able to enter the entire position. The price is aggressively driven up or down by aggressive market participants using their market orders.

- So, once the price has moved past the order block zone, it can be seen. It suggests that there was smart money buying or selling interest at the start of that move.

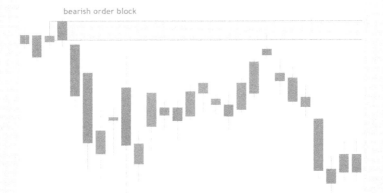

bearish order block

Why Does the Market Return to Order Block Zones That Have Not Been Tested?

- Given its size, the smart money position won't be filled entirely at once.
- The smart money was unable to complete all of its trades when the order block zone was established. If they enter the market quickly, the price moves with them. By doing this, they will be forced to buy higher and sell lower. They resolve this issue by continuing order blocks on the books.
- The purpose of leaving pending orders at order block zones is to allow the smart money to execute the trades they were initially unable to complete when the market moves back toward the order block zone. This enables the smart money to execute its remaining trades.
- on account of a Pending Block order.

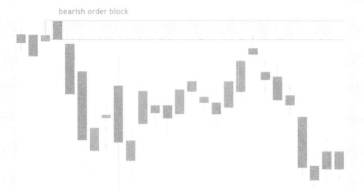

bearish order block

Criteria For Trading Order Block Zone That Is Valid

- A valid demand/supply zone is one where prices quickly move away from with wide candles (imbalance), structural or personality changes, and wide beaks. So, there are three key elements to research in order to identify a reliable zone.
- The order block zone is a liquidity hunting ground. For more information, visit the website.
- ☐Imbalances move or sharp move in a short time SRC/AR CANDLE MUST (MOVE AFTER OB).
- structure peaks/character changes (form 1 of 3 market structure).
- Untried order block zone FOR entry.

At the order block zone, looking for liquidity. IN THE FORM OF Stop Hunt Candle / Fake out/candle trap. Later, we'll go into more detail about this idea.

After The Order Block Zone, An Unbalanced Move.

When there is a large disparity between the volume of buy orders and sell orders for a given security or asset, this is referred to as an imbalance. This can happen when there is strong buying or selling pressure in the market, which can cause the security's price to move quickly in one direction.

1. If momentum should pick up speed. It signifies an imbalance in price.

2. Bullish order block previous candle low should not be breached in the following three candles, and order block zone should not be tested in the following three candles.

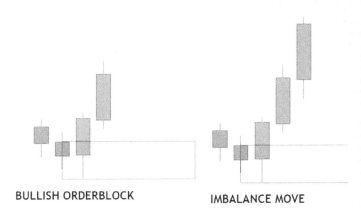

BULLISH ORDERBLOCK   **IMBALANCE MOVE**

With three consecutive candles making a higher high and higher low in the aforementioned example, there is a price imbalance. Now check the below example of price in balance. In this case, a balanced structure is formed after two candles.

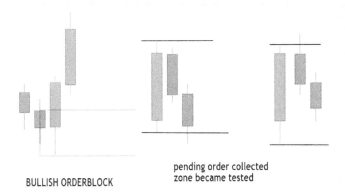

BULLISH ORDERBLOCK

pending order collected
zone became tested

AN EXAMPLE OF THE NIFTY 50 CHART IS PRESENTED BELOW.

IMBALANCE MOVE AFTER OB

Order Block Zone Trading Strategy For Volume.

If there is a high volume at a certain level, it may be a stronger level of support or resistance.

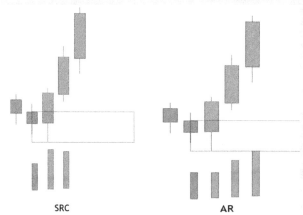

SRC   AR

Candle wands in the second example's low volume order block contrast with the first example's high volume order block to show how the volume can change. Both scenarios are Valid for OB..

THE CHART OF THE SAME NIFTY50 WITH THE VOLUME IS POSTED BELOW.

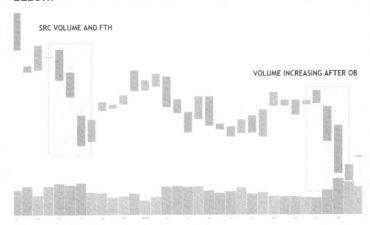

SRC VOLUME AND FTH

VOLUME INCREASING AFTER OB

Market Structure Ought To Be Broken By An Order Block Move.

break of structure

BULLISH STRUCTURE
BREAKOUT

BEARISH REVERSAL
BREAKOUT

__Understanding valid vs. invalid breakout is important before moving on.__

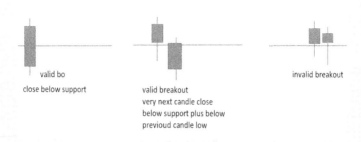

valid bo
close below support

valid breakout
very next candle close
below support plus below
previoud candle low

invalid breakout

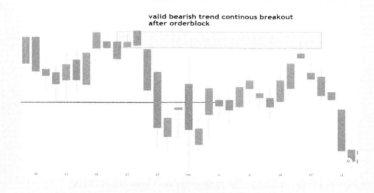

**valid bearish trend continous breakout
after orderblock**

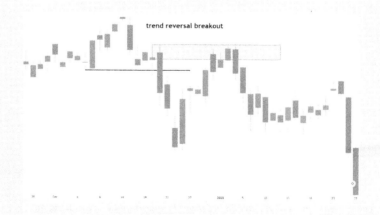

trend reversal breakout

Entry For An Untested OB.

I just prefer untested OB zones.

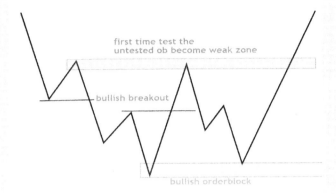

Market Structure Smart Money Trading Using Market Structure OB.

Smart money is the map that will make you understand where you are and what will happen next, including whether you are in continuation or correction We'll talk about the market structure now. Because we want to enter the controlling side, market structure typically determines who is in control. Liquidity and market structure are essentially supported by the smart money method.

The supply and demand dynamics can be significantly impacted by a large trader or institution taking a large position in a specific asset or market, which can change the price and direction of the market.

For instance, if a sizable institutional investor chooses to purchase a sizeable portion of shares in a specific company, this could increase demand and raise the price of the shares. Similar to the previous example, if a major trader takes a short position in a particular market, this may reduce demand and lower prices. identical to how we study trends.

1. Demand is in Control in an **UPTREND**
2. Supply is in control in a **DOWNTREND.**

Before Entering, We Consider The Following Three Things.

First Step
Know The Market Trend.
The first step in developing an order block-based trading strategy is to decide which market trend you want to trade. Examine the market's overall structure, which may include higher highs and higher lows or lower highs and lower lows. (Bearish or Bullish). We have a bias for trading opportunities because of market structure. We constantly look to buy during a bull market.

Second Step

Know And Identify Major OB Zones.

Finding significant or major bullish or bearish order block zones comes after identifying the market trend. These zones are places where the supply and demand are significantly out of balance. Depending on the higher timeframe trend, look for bullish or bearish order blocks. Therefore, if the higher timeframe trend is downward, you would search for a bearish order block, and if the market is bullish, you would search for a bullish order block.

Entry And Trade Management Is The Third Step.

Search for lower time frame confirmations while observing the lower time frames.

As can be seen, the market is downtrending, with lower lows and lower highs. Valid bearish OB formed but blocked. Keep an eye out for any bearish entries in the OB zone. The updated chart's is shown below.

So far, the summary.

1. who is in charge? market structure.

2. Order Block (point of entry).

Before beginning, it is important to understand some fundamental trends or market structure

The Principle Of Market Structure Smart Money In Order Block Trading.

The Movement of Price is within a structural Support and resistance. The breakout of any of these structure (resistance or support) will cause a price movement in the next region of the support or resistance.

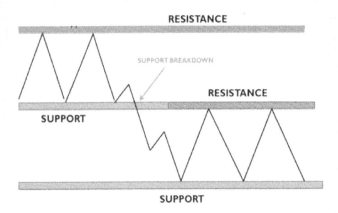

SL stands for Strong Low.

Market structure was high when the price broke. Eventually, the low point intensifies. The low that led to manipulation and the breakdown of structure (resistance) is known as a strong low.

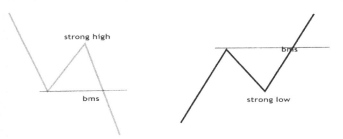

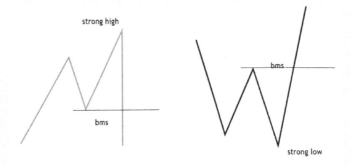

Low Weak or High Weak.

New highs in uptrends and new lows in downtrends. A weak low or high is one that fails to disrupt the structure *A WEAK HIGH OR LOW IS ALWAYS PRODUCED FROM A SOLID HIGH OR LOW*

- *A weak High follows every strong Low.*
- *There is a weak Low for each strong High.*

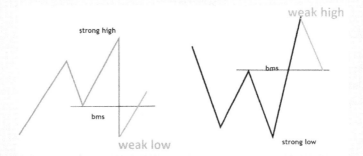

When Do Supply And Demand Break?

Eventually, Supply and Demand levels break when a zone is repeatedly tested or during a significant move. either because a large number of orders in the opposite direction break the level or because the last remaining orders are triggered and gradually removed.

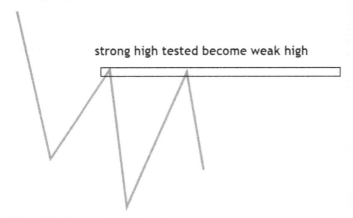

strong high tested become weak high

The Various Types Of Smart Money Market Structures Used In Order Block Trading.

Market Structure Phases

Price goes through these 4 Phases

- ACCUMULATION
- .UPTREND
- DISTRIBUTION
- DOWNTREND.

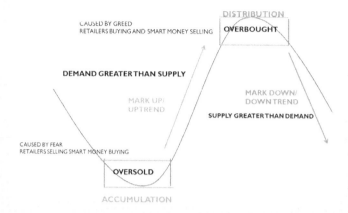

Based On The Entry Structure For Phase 3.

1. Market structure break during an uptrend or a downtrend.

2. A flip in supply-demand or a change in the nature of a trend reversal.

There are two trends: an upward trend and a downward trend.

We are biased by trend when looking for trading opportunities. We always look to buy dips during a bull market.

Uptrend – Price making
HH and HL

Break Of Market Structure.

Any time a candle breaks and closes outside of the structure (swing high in an uptrend and swing low in a downtrend), it is considered to have broken the structure and replaced it with a new one. Break of the structure created by the continuation of a trend.

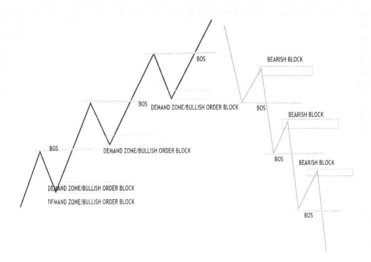

The fundamental steps for using the Continuous Order Block Entry Method are listed below.

<u>First Step</u>

Identify The Market Structure And Watch For Its Break.

By analyzing the price highs and lows, the market structure is identified. Finding the market you want to trade is the first step in developing an order block-based trading strategy. Look at the overall market structure, which may include higher highs and lower lows or vice versa. Positive or Negative).

We have a bias for trading opportunities because of market structure.

We constantly look to buy during a bull market.

Now traders needs to look for a market structure break. This might happen when the asset's price crosses a crucial support or resistance level or when it establishes a new high or low that is outside the bounds of the existing market structure. Trading Volume Should Rise To Confirm the Break In Market Structure Traders should also be on the lookout for a rise in trading volume. This can raise the likelihood of a profitable trade and offer additional evidence that a change in market sentiment is taking place.

Second Step

Recognize Potential Order Blocks

Now once immediately the market structure is broken, at ths point traders can search for potential order blocks. Order Blocks are the traces the market makes after an impulsive move. The Order Block (OB), which precedes the strong move that causes the market to become unbalanced, is the final opposite candle.

Finding major bullish or bearish order block zones comes after determining the market. The supply and demand are significantly out of balance in these zones. Look for a bullish order block or a bearish order block depending on the higher timeframe trend (for example, if the higher timeframe trend is down, you would look for a bearish order block, and if you are in a bullish market, you would look for a bullish order block).

Third Step

Take Positions or Leave Positions. (Enter or Exit)

Check the lower time frames and keep an eye out for any confirmations in the lower time frames. Following the market structure break, one order block was identified. Place a stop-loss order at an appropriate level to reduce potential losses in the event of a market reversal and enter the trade once the order block level has been confirmed. Manage the trade: After the position has been opened, watch it carefully. If necessary, adjust your stop-loss order and consider closing the position.

Any indicator can be used with the confluence factor for additional confirmation.

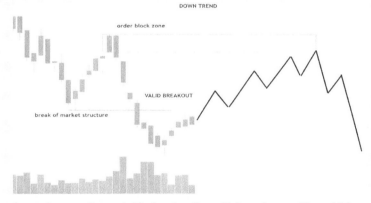

As can be seen, the market is downtrending, with lower lows and lower highs. Blocking a formed valid bearish order. Watch for any bearish entries in the OB zone. Below the updated chart, there is an OW check.

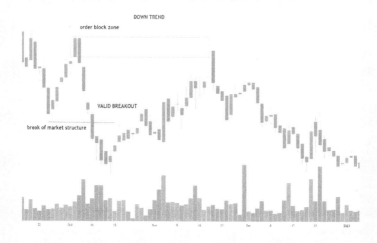

Here is another illustration.

Here is one more illustration.

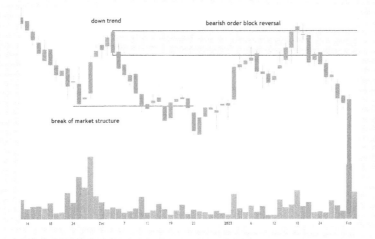

Change in Trend (Accumulation or Distribution).

Finding important supply and demand zones on a price chart and watching for a price flip or change in the trend at those zones to happen, which can indicate a potential reversal, are the key steps in this method. When this structure is broken, it can signal a change in market sentiment and present opportunities for traders to enter or exit positions.

A Trend Changes From Bearish To Bullish or Bullish to Bearish

- Stopping action or trend weakness.
- The strength of the trend shifts from being bearish to being bullish in terms of the candle and volume.
- Supply is being tested (whether it is present or not).
- Break of the market structure (if the supply-testing action turns up no supplies).

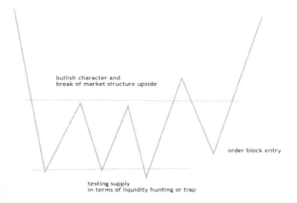

Let's start by going over each reversal market structure in detail.

Flipping Supply And Demand.

- Price established a new high (bullish demand was in charge given the market structure).
- It tested the previous demand zone (OB zone), but instead of buying, the price took a technical bounce from the demand zone and was unable to make a new higher high for the uptrend.
- It broke through the previous demand zone rather than making a higher high during the uptrend.
- We would sell when price retests the supply zone.

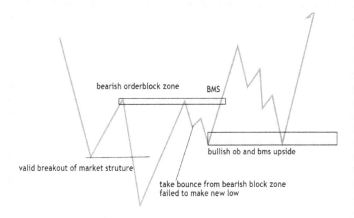

bearish orderblock zone

BMS

bullish ob and bms upside

valid breakout of market struture

take bounce from bearish block zone
failed to make new low

First Step

Identify The Market Structure (Including The Zone Of Supply And Demand).

1. Zones of key supply and demand identification: This is the first step. Demand zones are those where there is more buying pressure than selling pressure, while supply zones are those where selling pressure is more intense than buying pressure.

2. Once supply and demand zones have been established, watch for the price to enter one of these zones ***then wait for the zone to flip.***

- ***When the price reaches a supply or demand zone, watch for a price flip or change in the trend. A trend reversal could occur in which an upward trend turns downward or vice versa.***

Following that, traders should look for a break in the market's structure.

This might happen if the asset's price moves past a crucial support or resistance level or if it sets a new high or low that deviates from the established market structure. Trading Volume Should Rise To Confirm the Break In Market Structure. Traders should also be on the lookout for a rise in trading volume. This can raise the likelihood of a profitable trade and offer additional evidence that a change in market sentiment is taking place.

Second Step

Recognize Potential Order Blocks

Confirm the order block level: After the price flips, watch for evidence that the order block level has been confirmed by watching for a return to the level and a bounce off. When the market structure has been broken, traders can start searching for potential order blocks.

Whenever the market makes an impulsive move, order blocks are the tracks left behind. The Order Block (OB) is the final opposite candle before a significant move that upsets the market's equilibrium. Finding important bullish or bearish order block zones is the next step after identifying the market.

These zones are regions where the balance between supply and demand is noticeably off. Depending on the trend on the larger timeframe, look for bullish or bearish order blocks. As a result, you would search for a bearish order block if the higher timeframe trend is down, and a bullish order block if the market is up.

Third Step

Enter or Leave Positions.

Check the lower time frames and keep an eye out for any confirmations in the lower time frames. The market structure break has revealed one order block. Start trading: After the order block level has been confirmed, start trading in the direction of the order block. Set a stop-loss order at a suitable level to reduce potential losses in the event of a market reversal. Manage the trade: After the position has been opened, watch it carefully. If necessary, adjust your stop-loss order and consider closing the position. You can use the confluence factor as an indicator for more confirmation.

1. Enter the Trade: Once the order block level is confirmed, enter the trade in the direction of the price flip, placing a stop-loss order at an appropriate level to limit potential losses in the event of a market reversal.

2. **Manage the Trade:** Once the position is open, keep a close eye on it. If necessary, you should be ready to modify your stop-loss order and close the position.

Shift In Character.

1. BOF/TRAP. They encounter heavy supply, but instead of rebounding or reversing, the price broke the untested lower time frame demand zone, and each was close to the second demand zone.

2. AR BMS (STONG SUPPLY IN UPTREND) Supply in control, leaving a supply zone in its wake.

3. OB TESTING. We will sell when the price retests the supply zone.

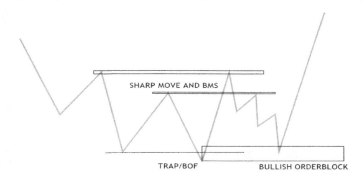

As the name implies, this pattern forms near a higher time frame supply/demand zone and involves changes in market sentiment and momentum by looking for changes in the structure of price action on a price chart.

- Determine the supply/demand areas that have not yet been tested on a higher time scale, then watch how the price moves around those areas. Keep an eye out for any indications that the nature or behavior of the price action has changed, such as a change in trend direction.
- Recognize possible order blocks: Order blocks are areas where sizable institutional traders may have placed buy or sell orders, causing significant price changes.
- Confirm the order block level after noticing a change in character by watching for the price to come back to the level, bounce off of it, or consolidate around it.
- Once the order block level is confirmed, place a stop-loss order at a suitable level to cap potential losses in the event of a market reversal and enter the trade in the direction of the change in character.
- Manage the trade: After the position has been opened, watch it carefully. If necessary, adjust your stop-loss order and consider closing the position.

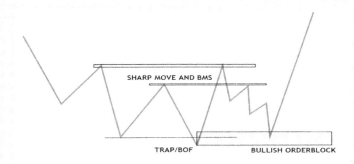

SHARP MOVE AND BMS

TRAP/BOF   BULLISH ORDERBLOCK

BEARISH BLOCK

SHARP MOVE AND BMS

BMS

BEARISH OB

SHARP MOVE   BMS

Trading utilizing the Institutional ORDER BLOCK Theory (ICT).

1. Use a higher TFs i to identify OBs. For instance, start with the Daily TF, followed by the H4 TF. The D1 and H4 TFs can be used to calculate your order flow (institutional trend).

2. You can now construct the OBs in lower TFs i because you have the institutional/directional bias for the long term. For instance, H1 and M15. Because that is where the real trend is going, M15, the entry TF, requires entries to follow the HIGHER TF Order Flow/Institutional bias.

3. When a price exceeds an earlier OB (We should wait for an (RTO) Return to Order Block) before entering if the close is above or below an OB. After breaking the OB, price should try again. The Last Step Broken Retest (LSB Retest) is a pattern that uses this method. You can trade the break without waiting for a retest, but you must be cautious because the broken OB could return.

We anticipate accepting taking trade from Source to Source using this Order Block Concept. i.e. Trading From one PEAK to another PEAK.

4. Integrated H4 I M15.
- **Monthly Chart: bearish.**
- **On the weekly chart, bearish.**
- **On the daily chart, bearish.**

The Lower TFs/Intraday charts H4, H1, and M15 will be correcting/retracing higher (i.e. producing Lower Highs). Here, you should look for buy side liquidity to sell to as you anticipate the price entering a premium (50 percent bullish retracement).

- Daily Chart = Bullish
- Weekly Chart = Bullish
- Monthly Chart = Bullish.

As a result, intraday charts with a time frame of four hours or less will correct or retrace lower (i. e. raising the lows). When this happens, you look for sell side liquidity to buy from because you expect the market to enter a discount (a 50% bearish retracement).

Institutional order block theory (ICT).

What exactly is an Institutional OB?
Order blocks are used in institutional trading.

A specific price range or candle known as the order block is where institutions will buy or sell against the retail trend or money dump.

Institutions reserve order blocks so that they can trade them later.

After hard-driving the price in the direction of the trend (the true institutional trend), they will reverse the price to a previous order.

We can also refer to these order blocks as specific levels of going long or short.
When an order block is broken or violated, it qualifies as a "breaker," which means that the price will retest that order block. It's sometimes referred to as a failed order block.

NOTE: You DO NOT TRADE ORDER BLOCKS DIRECTLY; RATHER, YOU WAIT FOR THE PRICE TO RETURN TO THAT ORDER BLOCK BEFORE YOU TAKE A TRADE.

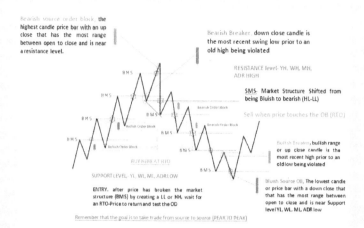

Bearish source order block, the highest candle price bar with an up close that has the most range between open to close and is near a resistance level.

Bearish Breaker, down close candle is the most recent swing low prior to an old high being violated

RESISTANCE level- YH, WH, MH, ADR HIGH

SMS- Market Structure Shifted from being Bluish to bearish (HL-LL)

Sell when price touches the OB (RTO)

Bullish Breaker, bullish range or up close candle is the most recent high prior to an old low being violated

Bluish Source OB, The lowest candle or price bar with a down close that that has the most range between open to close and is near Support level YL, WL, ML, ADR low

BMS

BMS

BMS

BMS

BMS

BMS

BMS

BMS

Bearish Order Block

Bullish Order Block

Bearish Finder Block

Bullish Order Block

BUY HERE AT RTO

SUPPORT LEVEL- YL, WL, ML, ADR LOW

ENTRY, after price has broken the market structure (BMS) by creating a LL or HH, wait for an RTO-Price to return and test the OD

Remember that the goal is to take trade from source to source (PEAK TO PEAK)

Types Of Order Blocks Include.

i. BUB (stands for Bullish Order Block)

ii. BEB (stands for Bearish Order Block)

The Order of Order Blocks

1. Source Order Block

2. Breaker Order Blocks.

3. continuation Order Block (basic Order Block/ Traditional Order Block)

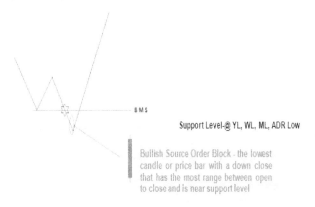

B M S

Support Level-@ YL, WL, ML, ADR Low

Bullish Source Order Block - the lowest
candle or price bar with a down close
that has the most range between open
to close and is near support level

The Lowest Candle or Price Bar with a Down Close, which has the Most
Range from Open to Close, and is Close to a "Support" level are considered
to be **Bullish Source Order Block**. Support levels for this Trend Reversal
Order Block include YL, WL, ML, and ADR Low. A Peak Formation Low I is
created by the final candle. e. least expensive price on the chart. So a Bullish
SOB denotes a change in the Market Structure from Bearish to Bullish.

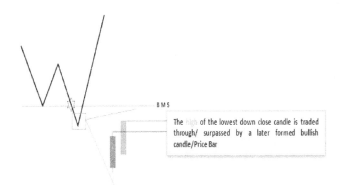

B M S

The high of the lowest down close candle is traded
through/ surpassed by a later formed bullish
candle/Price Bar

Validation Of a Bullish Source Order Block

When a later formed Candle or Price Bar trades through or surpasses the High of the Lowest Down Close Candle or Price Bar, this is evidence that a **Bullish SOB is Valid.**

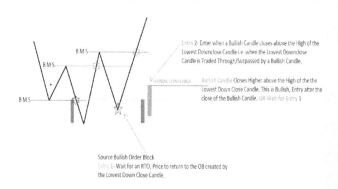

Entry 2- Enter when a Bullish Candle Closes above the High of the Lowest Downclose Candle i.e. when the Lowest Downclose Candle is Traded Through/Surpassed by a Bullish Candle.

Bullish Candle Closes Higher above the High of the the Lowest Down Close Candle. This is Bullish, Entry after the close of the Bullish Candle. OR Wait for Entry 1

Source Bullish Order Block
Entry 1- Wait for an RTO, Price to return to the OB created by the Lowest Down Close Candle.

Entry Methods: When Price Trades Higher Away From The Bullish Order Block And Then Returns To The Bullish Order Block Candle Or Price Bar High - This Is Bullish I. e. Then you enter after waiting for the price to RTO (Return to Order Block) or RTO. TO TRADE FROM ONE SOURCE TO ANOTHER IS THE GOAL.

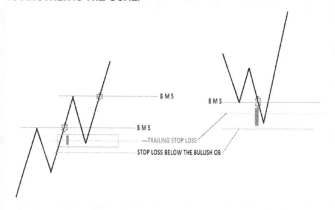

BMS

BMS

BMS

—TRAILING STOP LOSS

STOP LOSS BELOW THE BULLISH OB

Defining Risk

A comparatively secure Stop Loss is placed at the Low of the Bullish Order Block. When Price runs away from the Bullish Order Block, raising the Stop Loss at a point just below the 50% of the Order Block's total range is thought to be a good way to lower Risk.

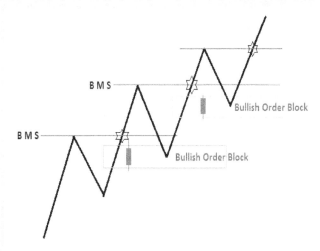

A Down Close candle with the greatest range between the open and close is known as a **_Bullish Order Block (BUB),_** and it is located in the most recent swing high. Institutions will make money in this area, for sure. For instance, selling against the trend and fresh market participants joining to continue the initial bullish trend.

A BUB is specifically the previous Bearish candle to an upward movement. The BUB is a series of institutional bullish orders (purchases) placed as the price was dropping (institutional buyers buy when the market declines).

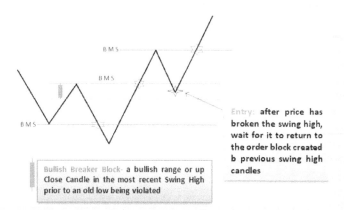

Entry: after price has broken the swing high, wait for it to return to the order block created b previous swing high candles

Bullish Breaker Block- a bullish range or up Close Candle in the most recent Swing High prior to an old low being violated

Bullish Break Block

A bullish range or Up Close Candle in the most recent Swing High before an Old Low is violated is known as a **Bullish Breaker Block.** Sellers who sold at this Low and later saw this Swing High broken will try to lessen their loss. This is a Bullish Trade Setup to consider if Price returns back to the Swing High.

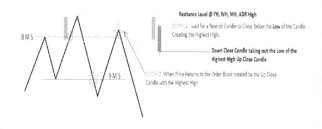

Resitance Level @ YH, WH, MH, ADR High

ENTRY 1 - wait for a Bearish Candle to Close Below the Low of the Candle Creating the Highest High.

Down Close Candle taking out the Low of the Highest High Up Close Candle

ENTRY 2: When Price Returns to the Order Block created by the Up Close Candle with the Highest High.

Bearish Source Order Block- the Highest Candle or price bar with an Up-close that has the most range between open to close and is near Resistance Level.

A **Bearish Source Order Block** is the highest candle or price bar with an up-close, the greatest range from open to close, and is located close to a resistance level. The resistance level could be the YH, WH, MH, or ADR High. This is a Trend Reversal Order Block. Peak Formation High was created by this last candle, for instance, the highest price point shown on the chart. An indication of a shift in market structure (SMS) from bullish to Bearish Is a Bearish Sob.

A bearish SOB is considered valid when a later formed Candle or Price Bar trades through or surpasses the Low of the Highest Up Close Candle or Price Bar.

Entry Techniques: Wait for price to return to the bearish source order block (RTO-Return to Order Block/Origin) before entering when price trades lower away from the bearish order block and then returns to the bearish order block candle or price bar high. THE GOAL IS TO TRANSACT FROM ONE SOURCE TO ANOTHER.

Determining Risk: A relatively secure Stop Loss is placed at the high of the bearish source order block. When the price has moved away from the bearish order block, it is thought to be a good idea to raise the stop loss just above the 50% mark of the order block's total range to minimize risk.

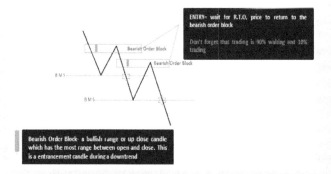

Bearish Order Block- a bullish range or up close candle which has the most range between open and close. This is a entrancement candle during a downtrend

In the most recent swing low, the candle with the most range between the open and close is called a "B**earish OB" (BEB).**

A BEB is specifically the final bullish candle in a downtrend, following a bearish movement, or a series of bullish candles.

The BEB is a collection of sell orders placed by institutions in a bearish manner as the price increased (institutions typically sell when the market increases).

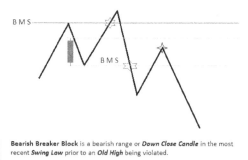

Bearish Breaker Block is a bearish range or *Down Close Candle* in the most recent *Swing Low* prior to an *Old High* being violated.

ENTRY- Wait for R T O, Price to Return to the Bearish Breaker Block.

A Bearish Breaker Block is a bearish range or Down Close Candle in the most recent Swing Low before an Old High is violated.

The buyers who purchase at this low and later observe that the same swing low has been broken will try to lessen their loss.

This is a Bearish Trade Setup to take into account when Price Reverses to the Swing Low.

An Introduction To Trading With Order Flows.

Order Flow Trading What is It?

Order flow trading, to put it simply, is a style of trading that focuses on comprehending how orders enter the market as a result of traders' decisions.

Order flow trading has been around since the beginning of contemporary financial markets, though not in the form that we would recognize today. It is not a new way to trade the forex markets.

The term "order flow" refers to the manner in which buy and sell orders "flow" into the market as a result of various market participants making trading-related decisions, such as opening and closing positions and taking profits. In all other financial markets, order flow trading would be carried out using an indicator known as the order.

The order book is a trading indicator that provides the trader using it with a wealth of information regarding the buy and sell orders coming into the market from the various financial institutions.

It displays the prices at which buy and sell orders are being made, the categories of orders that are actually being made (i.e. e market orders or pending orders) as well as the size of the orders themselves.

The order book, for those who have access to it, offers a significant advantage over other kinds of market analysis, though, as with anything in trading, it does require a lot of training to learn how to use it effectively.

Unfortunately, because there is no centralized exchange where trading takes place, we cannot use the order book in the forex market.

Order Flow Trading's Differences From Other Types Of Trading.

To establish what order flow trading is and isn't when compared to practices like price action trading, I believe it's crucial to briefly discuss the differences order flow trading has with other trading styles.

In that they both advocate analyzing the market in a particular way, order flow trading and price action trading are types of trading that are comparable to one another. While order flow traders believe they can predict where the market is going to move by simply understanding the actions made by the traders in the market, price action traders believe they can predict where the market is going to move by analyzing the market price.

If you were to ask me which type of trader I believe I am, I would respond that I consider myself to be a combination of the two because I use order flow trading principles in addition to the standard tools used by price action traders, such as pin bars, support and resistance levels, and Fibonacci retracements.

For instance, using my knowledge of order flow trading, I can predict when a pin bar has most likely formed as a result of bank traders taking profits from their trades. Because I know which pins are likely to cause the market to reverse and which are going to fail, having this knowledge enables me to make more profitable pin bar trades.

How Do Order Flow Trades Work?

The theory behind order flow trading is that by anticipating when and where traders are likely to make trades, you can predict with a high degree of accuracy which way the market will move. The reason why is that each time a trader makes a choice—to open or close a position, for example—they place an order in the market that could potentially result in price subject to change.

A price change cannot be brought about by a single order, but it can be brought about by thousands of orders entering the market simultaneously.

An order flow trader's primary objective is to comprehend how other market participants trade because doing so will help him predict when a significant number of orders will likely enter the market and drive the price up or down. Since there are so many different trading strategies available, it can be challenging to determine how other traders trade.

Fortunately, we don't need to understand the specifics of trading methods employed by individuals. To determine when and where they will make a decision that will place orders in the market, all we need to know is what their trading strategy's fundamental objective is.

There are primarily two categories of trading strategies used by investors in the forex market:.

1. Trend trading strategies
2. Reversal trading strategies.

Trend Trading Strategies
The goal is getting the trader using trend trading strategies into a trading position after a movement in the market has already taken place. A great illustration of this is a moving average system, which only crosses its averages after the market has moved up or down for some time.

Reversal trading strategies.
Reversal trading strategies now aim to place the trader into a position PRIOR TO a market movement. Reversal trading strategies include things like looking for candlestick patterns at support and resistance levels or entering trades at supply and demand zones. Both strategies aim to get the trader using them into a trade before a movement in the market has taken place, despite the fact that they are quite different from one another.

Consequently, despite the fact that there are numerous variations of trend trading and reversal trading strategies, they are all essentially just different interpretations of the same basic idea. Either before a movement has occurred or after a movement has occurred, they are attempting to convince a trader to enter a trade.

Understanding these two facts alone eliminates the need to learn the intricate details of every single trading strategy available because you already know when the traders employing these strategies are likely to enter the market and place their trades. i.e either before or a after a market movement has occurred.

Order Flow Trading Basics

Now, let's quickly review some of the fundamental order flow ideas you should be familiar with if you plan to use order flow analysis to trade the forex market.

Understanding How Various Orders Affect Market Price.

Even though different traders' trading decisions ultimately determine how much the price moves, it is the orders that result from these decisions that drive the market's price up and down. An important aspect of being an order flow trader is understanding these orders and the various effects they have on the market price. This will help you better understand why the market moves the way it does.

There are two types of orders that traders can carry out in the market. These two orders are executed by traders for various reasons, and their executions each have a different impact on the market price.

Let's look at the nature of these orders.

Market Orders.

A trader who wants to get a trade into the market as soon as possible will use a market order. A trader will use a market order to enter a trade to make sure he doesn't miss an opportunity to make money when he notices something happening on his charts that he defines as a chance to do so right away.

Reactive trading strategies are those in which the trader enters a trade using a market order as a response to what he observes happening in the market at the moment.

Limit orders and Pending orders.

The orders that traders use to have a trade placed at a price that hasn't yet been reached in the market are pending orders and limit orders. In contrast to traders who use market orders, these traders prefer to execute their trades at a later time. Stop losses are similar to limit orders in that they guarantee that you will buy or sell currency at a price that the market hasn't yet reached when they are placed.

The stop loss itself is a limit order to sell or buy at a price that hasn't yet been reached, so when you place a trade using a market order that has a stop loss, you are essentially placing two orders into the market.

The use of limit orders to enter trades is referred to as a predictive strategy because the limit order is set at a price in the market where the trader anticipates a future event will occur.

The impact they have on the market price is the primary distinction between market orders and pending or limit orders. A market order uses up some of the liquidity that is present in the market, whereas a pending or limit order adds liquidity to the market.

Example:.

Consider that if you were trading USD/JPY, the bid price, at which you could sell, would be 112.100, and the offer price, at which you could buy, would be 112.098.

Let's assume that the best offer at 112.998 is 13 million sell orders and the best bid at 112.100 is 7 million buy orders. This indicates that there are 10 million limit orders to sell at 112.998 and 7 million limit orders to buy at 112.100. The 13 million limit orders to sell must be filled by 13 million or more market orders to buy for the market to move upward.

When that takes place, the market will increase to the price at which the subsequent best offer has been made. The price would increase from 112.098 to 112.120 if, as an example, the next best offer was 15 million limit orders to sell at 112.120.

There would be insufficient sell side liquidity in the market as it moved from 112.098 to 112.120 because there are no buyable sell limit orders until the market reaches 112.120. Therefore, the 10 million limit orders to sell provided buy side liquidity because they allowed traders to use market orders to buy at 112.098 until the 10 million limit orders to sell were used up.

If the market were to decline from 112.100, the opposite would also have to occur.

If there were 7 million limit buy orders at 112.100, the market could only fall from this price if there were 7 million or more market sell orders. The price will drop to the level where the next best bid has been placed if those orders are received. The market would drop to that price before stopping if the next best offer was to purchase 20 million at 112.090.

There is a lack of buy side liquidity when the price is dropping to this level because there are no limit orders available to buy until the price reaches the 112.090 level. within this.

For instance, the 7 million limit orders to buy provided sell side liquidity because they allowed the traders using market orders to sell the opportunity to sell at 112.100 until the 7 million limit orders to buy were consumed.

You observe what I've just described taking place on your charts every single day.

When you observe a price change in the market, it is because all limit orders that were present at that price were satisfied by new market orders coming from traders looking to execute trades. However, the fundamental process is still the same: the price won't change until all limit orders at that price have been filled by market orders. Of course, things move much more quickly in real markets, and the size of the orders would likely be much larger than what I've listed above.

Liquidity.

When learning about order flow trading, liquidity is a crucial concept you'll hear a lot.

The term "liquidity" refers to how simple it is to buy or sell something on the market. If a market is said to be very liquid, it means that buying and selling there is relatively simple. Not-liquid would indicate that buying and selling is very challenging. Due to how simple it is to locate buyers and sellers, the forex market is regarded as one of the most liquid financial markets in the world. Despite being one of the most liquid markets, it still experiences high and low liquidity periods (illiquidity).

I've highlighted the move up in orange for you to see.

Because it was so difficult for bank traders to place sell orders during this up-move, movements like this are regarded as low liquidity up-moves. Due to a lack of sellers in the market, the majority of orders that entered the market during this move up were buy orders, which means that the banks were unable to execute any of their own buy trades.

What they can do is carry out an action that needs a lot of buy orders to enter the market. The banks can take actions during up-moves like these, as they can only be completed when there are a large number of buy orders entering the market, such as placing sell trades or taking profits off of already existing buy trades.

Here is a picture of the USD/JPY downmove during a low liquidity period.

Since all of the orders entering the market at the time of this downward movement were sell orders from traders selling, it would have been extremely challenging for the banks to place sell trades. Since both of these actions require that a significant number of sell orders enter the market, it would have been simple for them to place buy trades or take profits off any sell trades they have already placed.

What i want you to take away from all of this is that, whenever you see a low liquidity movement end, it means that the bank traders have taken a position in the market. To know what they decided depends on the direction the low liquidity movement happened at.

In the event of a downward trend, as shown in the image above, you would be aware that the banks' traders had either entered buy trades into the market or had taken a profit off of sell trades that had already been entered.

If it was an uptrend, you would know it because they would have either placed sell trades or taken profits off of buy trades, which can only happen when there are many buy orders available.

Time is another factor that significantly affects the level of market liquidity.

When markets are active, it is simple to buy or sell currencies because many traders are actively participating in the market and making trading decisions. Additionally, there are a lot of bank traders making decisions in the market, which means that bank traders can interact with one another to place trades or profit from trades. The markets are busiest when the traders who deal in each currency are available.

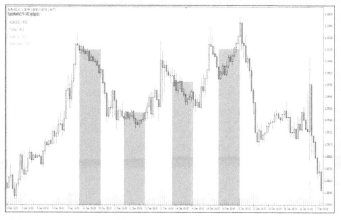

When these sessions end, there are fewer traders in the market making trades, which results in a decrease in market liquidity.You can see how the activity is doing if you go to MT4 and choose the volume tool. When the main trading periods for the currency you're viewing end, the market starts to decline significantly.

I've highlighted some of the periods in the image above where there was little activity on the EUR/USD.

If you pay close attention, you'll notice that the end of the US trading session coincides with the moment when activity really slows down and begins to base out. (10:00pm GMT for those who don't know) It always picks back up again around 8:00 - 9:00am in the morning, just as the London trading session is starting to get going. This pattern will be present on every currency available on the market. The volume (activity) will increase when the main trading sessions for the currency you are viewing start, and it will decline and level out as they end.

The Banks How Do They Trade

One of the key elements of order flow trading is comprehending how large groups of retail traders trade, but you also need to comprehend how bank traders trade since they will ultimately be the ones driving up and down movements in the market price. The way the banks trade is very different from the way we retail traders trade, as you might expect. Not necessarily in terms of the trading strategies they actually employ, but rather in terms of the prerequisites that must exist before they can execute trades or realize profits.

We never consider whether or not there are sufficient orders entering the market to allow us to execute our trade when deciding to place one. This is due to the fact that we are aware we can make trades whenever we like. We are putting very small trades into the market, which makes this possible.

When we want to place our trade, there only needs to be a very small number of buy or sell orders entering the market. Now, regrettably, the banks do not enjoy this luxury because their trade sizes are significantly larger than ours.

They are only able to place trades when there are a large number of buy orders (or sell orders, if they were placing sell trades) entering the market. Because most orders entering the market are buy orders from traders placing buy trades of their own, this means that when an up-move occurs, the banks are unable to get buy trades placed or take profits off any sell trades. What they can do is place sell trades or profit from active buy trades, which both require a significant number of buy orders to enter the market.

It works the other way around for down-moves. The majority of the orders entering the market when the market is falling are sell orders from people selling and liquidating losing buy trades, so the banks are unable to place sell trades or decide to take profits off any buy trades they have placed. They can choose to take profits from their existing sell trades or place some buy trades into the market, as these two actions can only be carried out if there are many sell orders entering the market.

Slippage.

When your trade is placed at a price other than the one you wanted it to be placed at, it is referred to as slippage.

When bank traders place a trade that is larger than the volume of new orders entering the market, slippage occurs. In other words, if I entered the market and made a purchase of 4 million AUD when there were only 3 million orders to sell AUD, 3 million of my buy orders would be filled immediately, but the remaining million wouldn't be filled until after another 1 million orders to sell entered the market.

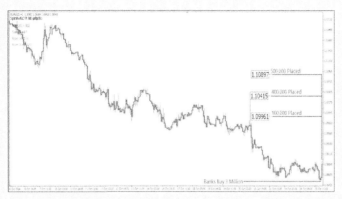

Here is an illustration of what happens when slippage occurs in a trade for a bank trader.

You can see how the banks place their 3 million buy orders at the lowest price. The market then moves higher to look for more sell orders to match the one million buy orders the banks still have available to place in the market. The end result is that it discovers 100,000 sell orders at 1.09961, leaving the banks with 900,000 buy orders to place.

A short while later, another 400,000 sell orders are discovered at 1.1041, as the price continues to rise. The price is currently increasing because the banks still have 500,000 buy orders that haven't been fulfilled. The market eventually receives 500,000 sell orders, and the remaining 1.10897 buy trades are entered by bank traders.

Slippage makes bank traders' profits from their trading positions less profitable, which is why it is such a major problem for them. In our example, because there weren't enough sell orders entering the market at the time the banks decided to place their buy trade, only a portion of their buy position was placed at the price they actually wanted it to be placed at. The rest of their trades were executed at much higher prices, so the bank traders would not have profited as much from these trades had all of their trades been executed at the same price.

51

Order Splitting

The bank traders get their trades placed at prices that are close to one another in order to prevent slippage on their trades. Order splitting is a technique used to accomplish this. In order to make it simpler for them to get their entire trade executed in the market at the prices they want, bank traders will split up one very large trade into many smaller trades.

As an illustration:.

Let's assume that the banks desired to execute a buy trade on the AUD/USD pair worth $7 million. They would need 7 million sell orders to enter the market in order for them to place the entire buy trade. The issue is that, at the time they want to place their trade, there are only 1 million sell orders available in the market.

The banks could simply go ahead and enter their entire 7 million buy position into the market, but doing so would result in slippage. Instead, they divide the 7 million buy position into numerous smaller trades, which makes it simpler for them to enter their entire position into the market without experiencing any slippage.

Look at the AUD/USD reversal that just happened.

This is a perfect illustration of the banks breaking up a very large trade into smaller, more manageable sizes to ensure that the entire trade is placed at advantageous prices.

If we apply the illustration I just gave to this chart, you can see that each swing low was created as a result of the bank traders selling 1 million of their total 7 million buy positions. They would have had slippage and a lot of their buy trades would have ended up being placed at progressively worse prices if they had simply placed their entire 7 million buy position without there being enough sell orders available.

The bank traders can have much more control over when and where their buy trades are placed by segmenting their position. In order to ensure that they all make the same amount of profit when the market starts to move up, this enables them to place their trades at prices that are close to one another.

Order Block Refinement in a Lower Timeframe.

The first thing we must do with OBs is to reduce them whenever possible. It is crucial for us to understand where the market's momentum has come from. meaning the places where the institutions have already entered. Because of the fact that price usually returns to the area where momentum first began to slow down before continuing its movement, whether it be upward or downward, that area is where momentum usually starts.

Refining OBs down on LTF is advantageous to us because it tightens our AOI, allowing us to enter trades with tighter stop losses and typically lowering drawdown. Additionally, it will give us the opportunity to raise the return rate (RR) on our trades, enabling us to generate a higher return.

This example shows a 1hr bullish order block. The distance from the low is 10 pips

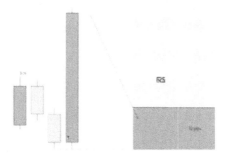

Bringing it down to a lower time frame (15mins) observe how we are able to refine our order block zone and decrease our area

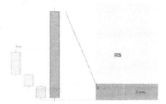

The examples demonstrate OB refinement. Let's start with the fact that this indicates a 1 hour time frame bullish OB. The last down candle before the BOS's upmove was the BOS, so we had this BOS. We take the high and the low, so this would be our OB. So, 10 pip is where our stop is set.

As we can see, if we switch from a 1 hour time frame to a 15 minute time frame, we might see something like this. Look at the way we can refined our OB and reduce our area.

This is what we can see on the 1h chart, and yes, I am aware that there are only three candles, but when we zoom out to the 15m chart, we can see exactly where the market momentum is entering. This candle in this example, which is also a BOS, represents the last downward movement, which on a 15-minute chart could be 5 pip-sized.

Therefore, 10 pips for a 1hour Oder Block refined down to 15minutes to 5 pips.

What Does This Mean For Our Entry And Stop Loss Now?

We can enter a trade with a stop loss that is obviously half the size, which results in greater accuracy, increased return on investment (RR), and possibly reduced drawdown. This is exactly what LTF refinement means.

So a bullish OB refinement will be the first example we'll look at.

Zooming in on the 1-hour chart reveals that there was a high, a pullback, and then a BOS. So, with a clear OB in front of us, we insert a new HH. So we take the last down move before the BOS.

If we were to enter based solely on this, we would do so at the top with our stop loss placed at the bottom, giving us 11 pip profit.

last down candle
but not engulfed
the OB

Last candle before
momentum

Now, if we were to try to narrow it down, this would be the 15m. This is how the 1h OB appears to us right now on 15m.

Can we make it more precise? The momentum has clearly entered on this candle, so let's look at where it came from. The size and importance of this candle are apparent. We can now narrow our 1h OB down by determining where the most recent down candle is, if it is this one or the one before it, but if we take the next candle, the OB has not yet been engulfed. Let's refine it to this candle, which essentially reduces our stop loss, which was over here on 1h at 11 pips, to 6 pips.

As a result, if we look at where the price is, we can see that we tapped into the market exactly. Here, we would be running at 11 points 15 RR, and over the 1 hour OB, we would be running at about 5 points 6 RR.

We can therefore see that, simply by comprehending refinement and learning how to be more precise, we have effectively doubled our return.

Can We Go One Step Further With This Then?

refine even more
to this doji

Yep. We can take it a step further and consider this as our OB here. If we look at the subsequent candle, as we can see that it is a small doji candle that isn't showing any momentum and hasn't yet engulfed the OB.

As we can see, price impulsed up, and will returned and tapped in to further define our zone. Thus, theoretically, we are able to set a stop loss at 3.5pips..

Do I still recommend it?

Not exactly, reason being that we still have the low we used to mark our OB, which means we can still account for the low. However, the idea still holds true: we precisely timed our taps to coincide with the start of the upward momentum.

In other words, if we can narrow it down to this candle, we are looking at 3.5 pip spread, and our trade would run just short 19 percent in one candle. Therefore, refinement has great power, and it's important to watch the market to see where momentum is entering.

1hour

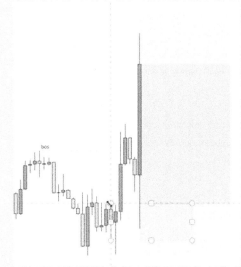

15m

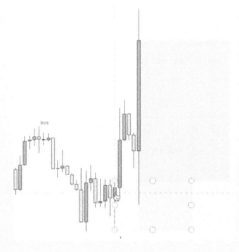

Let's move on to another example in the EU. As you can see, we made a quick move up above the structure starting at the one hour. Giving us an OB to work with as a result.

So before the up move, we had this final downward movement, but the subsequent candle did not. exhibited no momentum, and it did not engulf the OB.

So, we refine it down. As a result, the area we have to work with is larger in this instance because we have a large wick. So, deciding which candle to use ultimately depends on personal preference.

Since this is the final move in this consolidation before the expansion out, we will now take this refined. We can see that we BOS and pulled back before tapping in and moving upward.

Here, if we calculate from the high and low, we are running about 2.8RR. And looking at 17.6 pips

1hour

15m

What do we have on 15m? The final down move with a sizable wick that expanded out of this consolidation range. We tapped back in after that, but we can still get more refinement with this. The stop loss would be 14 pip if we simply assumed that we entered with a limit order as the price came back in, but we can still refine it down even further.

Therefore, since we haven't shown any real momentum, we can take this candle and look at the following one. However, since we can see that the next candle is when we actually got a breakout of this range, the momentum came in on this candle, this is the candle that we should be looking at to take.

Thus, this enables us to lower our stop loss from 14 pip to as little as 6 pip.

Now, it goes without saying that we should account for a few pip changes, but let's move forward with this for the time being. Therefore, it is clear that we tapped in precisely, but we should now move to the upside.

Due to the ability to refine the previous candle OB to 6 pip increments, we were able to increase our profit from 4.8RR to 10.3RR.

As a result, we can see the effectiveness of this refinement. However, placing entries blindly without confirmation when the price changes would be risky.

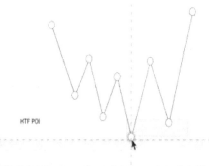

HTF POI

We will now discuss how to wait for additional information. A quick tip on what we look for is that once price taps in on a 1h or 15m OB into the OB, we can drop to a LTF like 5m or 1m, or even a 30s, and what we are looking for is essentially priced to tap in just like this and then show us the BOS.

We would like to see it on a LTF, just like we have here where we are aware of the price being BOS. Therefore, we want to see a nice impulse up that looks just like this. We can see that the structure above was broken because we had this LL, LH, a BOS, and, let's just say, this is a HTF POI or OB.

We tapped in, and now we want to see the LTF BOS, which will cause an OB on the LTF. In contrast to making riskier entries, this provides us with much more confirmation. We are anticipating the price's move, and once we have this BOS, we can enter without a doubt.

We have a very tight stop loss, which is how we can enter a trade with a stop loss of just one, two, or three pip and still have a great return on trades (RR).

The following example is essentially the same as the previous one, but I want to emphasize this idea as much as I can because it is so effective. Now that we have one hour, the move was started from this point because we had just impulsed up BOS.

We can easily narrow it down to this candle here even though we have the most recent downward move. Therefore, we have an OB of 15,8 pips

As a result, after we pushed off , we could set our entry and would have been tagged on this candle. We would now need a stop loss that was at least 15 points seven pip high. We can see that after being tapped in once, twice, and again, we pushed off, but after that, we came back in to push lower before we pushed off and BOS.

The stop loss size of 15.7 pips is currently very large, so let's see how we can reduce it on the 15m.

Now that this move is just on the 15m, we can see that this is where the last downward movement occurred, on this doji. Therefore, the momentum entered on the following candles, which also broke above this high, indicating that this is the final downward movement. Therefore, it is likely that the price will return to this area and possibly decrease to this point; however, it may arrive at this point and then continue..

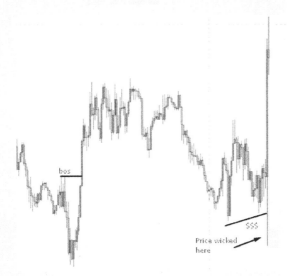

So let's wait and see what transpires. We'll start now. Furthermore, from these lows, we built some liquidity. Now that we can see that price did wick in, it is likely that news played a role in this. However, news is simply a tool used by large institutions to enter the market and drive prices lower in order to offset and close out any sell positions we may have before stacking orders and continuing.

Therefore, if we were to set our entry on the 15m OB, that is where we would be looking at our entry. We have a 5 pip stop loss, so it is clear that we were able to decrease the size of our stop loss from 1h, which was 15 pip, to 15m, which is 5 pip. Consequently, our stop loss was lowered by 10 pips, which will ultimately result in a much higher return on investment (RR) on trades.

Therefore, we can see that from higher up, we are looking at 11RR, while on the 1hour, we have 3RR.

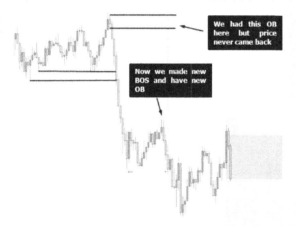

We are currently looking at a sell example on the AU, so we are searching for refinements in the bearish OB. Now that we have made a very impulsive downward move that has destroyed a lot of structure, we would have an OB up here that we could examine, but as we looked at what the price had done, we pulled back and then we bos again, creating another OB. As a result, even though we already have bos, price may not necessarily need to rise to the first OB.

This could therefore be applied at a later time. As a result of our position, the final bullish candle before the downward movement is the bearish OB.

If we were to look at entering, our limit order would have been tagged in at this point and our stop loss would have needed to be 12 pip. The low that is currently present or immediately below it should be our primary focus. So, 5RR to the low is what we are looking at.

But if we shift our focus to the 15m once more, we can see the same movement as in the 1h, but we can also be refined down.

So, if we look at the 1h, we see these wicks. Now, when we see wicks at the top or bottom like this, it essentially indicates an AOI on LTF. So, that's it for the 15m.

We can refine it down to this candle because we haven't shown the momentum when we have this move to the downside, which bos as well, and when we have the last bullish up move before the down move. Our refined OB is thus this.

As a result, the 1 hour OB now has 7 pip instead of 12 pip.

And after that, it becomes clear that the price was locked in, the OB was mitigated to 50%, and momentum was then generated.

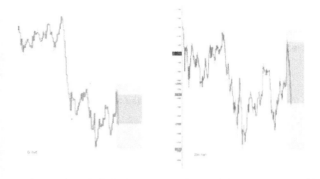

Now that it has been refined down, we have almost 9RR to the low instead of 5RR from 1h. Therefore, just to the low, we have nearly doubled our return.

Market Structure Cheat Sheet

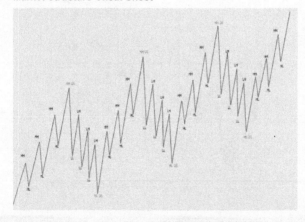

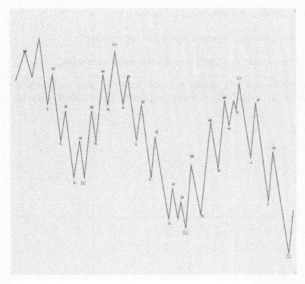

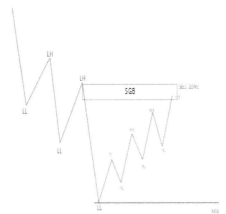

STEP 1.
Study the market structure on the longer time frames (W, D, and H4).
STEP 2.
Find out what the upcoming Structure (e. g. LH).
STEP 3.

Find any OB or OBIM in the important DP in the HTF.
STEP 4.
Visit the LTF, examine the structure, and search for OBIM.
STEP 5.
In the M5-M1 charts, look for OBIM to enter the trade after BOS.
STEP 6.
Watch the price on the LTF while you wait to enter (you can enter a pending order if you'd like). Put in a pending order if your OBIM is on the M1 chart.

BOS

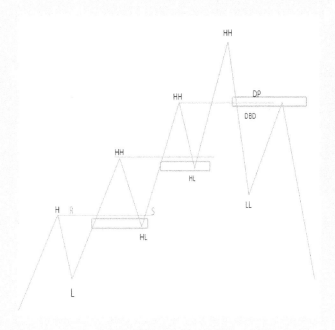

Price Coming to (PA)

1. CPLQ
2. Flippy
3. Accumulation or Distribution
4. Diamond

<u>No GO, NO PA</u>

30% will be PA risk

If there is no PA risk will be between 60% - 90%

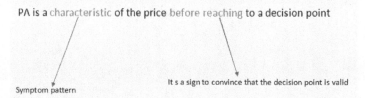

PA is a characteristic of the price before reaching to a decision point

Symptom pattern

It s a sign to convince that the decision point is valid

Theory of waves.

Advice: Instead of viewing the market as candles, think of it as lines.

Cycles typically consist of 5 moves (3 Impulses and 2 Pullbacks/Corrections).

Once a full wave cycle has finished, a NEW wave cycle may begin.

Make sure that every TF is correlating with one another. Inside of 1 wave, you can see a complete market cycle in LTF.

Harmonic Patterns are the 4th and 5th Wave (at the end of the Trend).

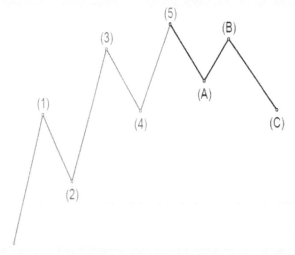

Five wave and 3 wave pattern (Dominant trend and corrective trend)

Because the market is fractal, waves within waves can be seen on shorter timescales. Although we don't use Elliott waves, it's important to remember that the market is fractal in nature.

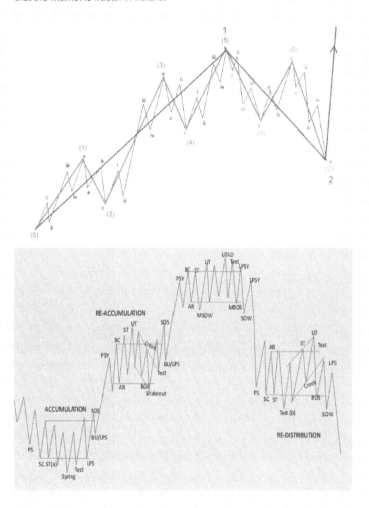

First Accumulation

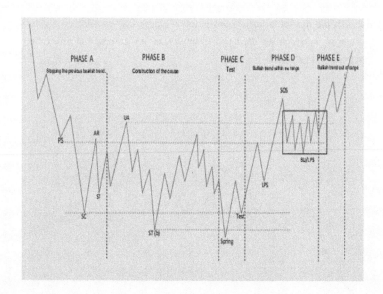

SECOND ACCUMULATION WITH NO SPRING

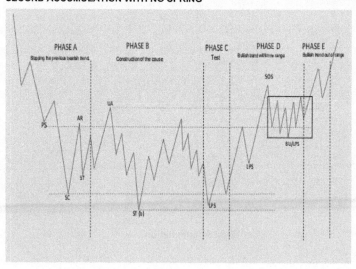

Schematic Accumulation No3

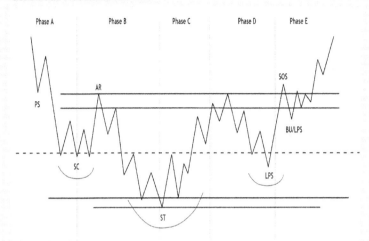

ACCUMULATION DESCENDING WEDGE

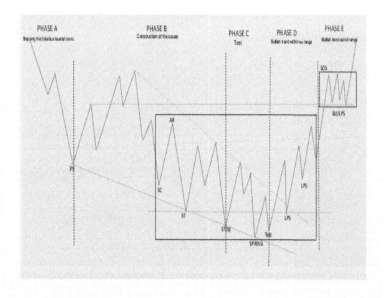

Schematic DISTRIBUTION No1

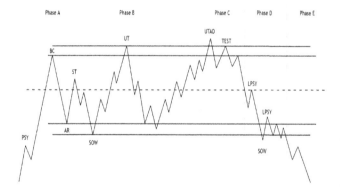

Schematic DISTRIBUTION No2

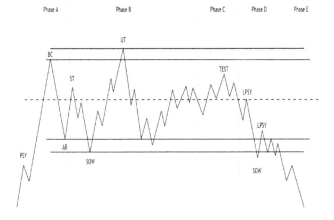

Schematic DISTRIBUTION No3

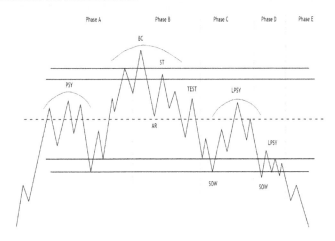

Schematic DISTRIBUTION No4

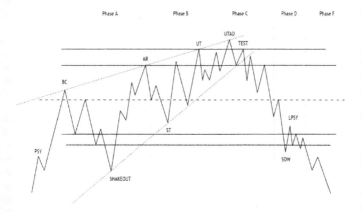

Re-accumulation Schematic No1

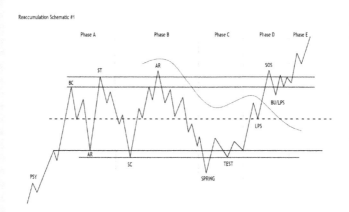

Reaccumulation Schematic #1

Re-accumulation Schematic No2

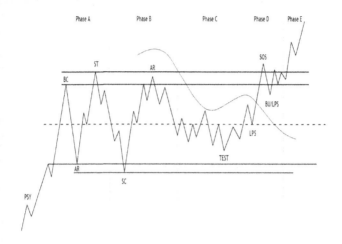

Re-accumulation Schematic No3

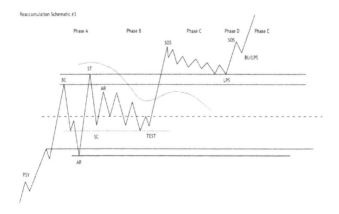

Re-accumulation Schematic No4

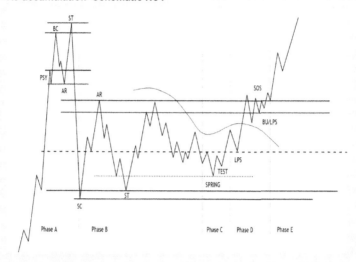

Redistribution Schematic No1

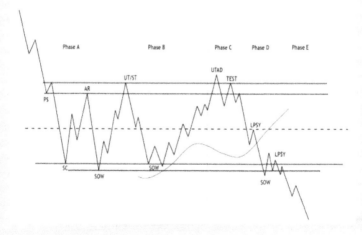

Redistribution Schematic No2

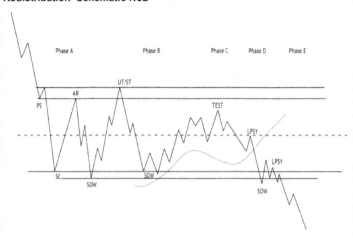

Redistribution Schematic No3

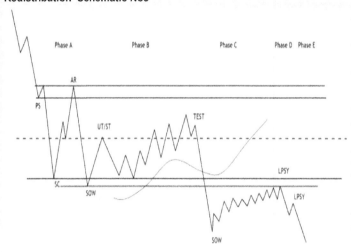

Redistribution Schematic No4

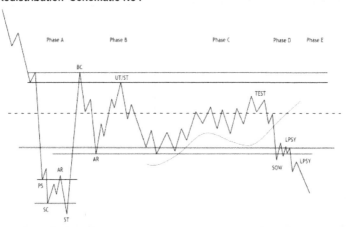

Deciding Candlesticks

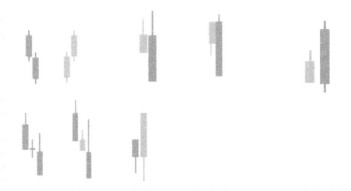

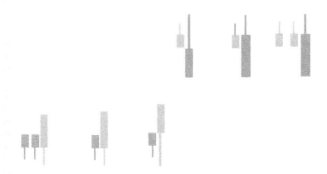

Weakening Base, or WD.

Before SDE occurred, the base was weakening.

In accordance with WB regulations, the SD is subject to multiple rejection, the head is descending (SDP), and the PA will accumulate (my personal favorite).

SDP is the DP that manages to keep the price steady while the price fails to generate a new HH.

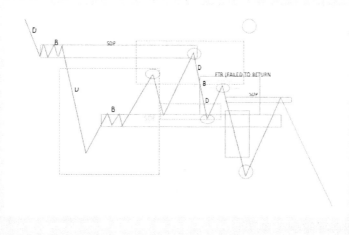

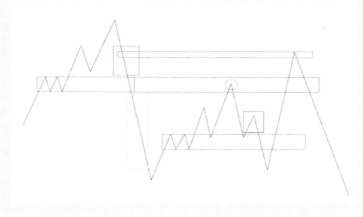

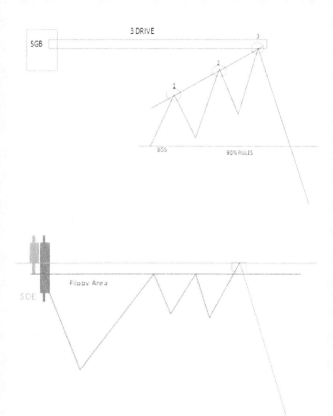

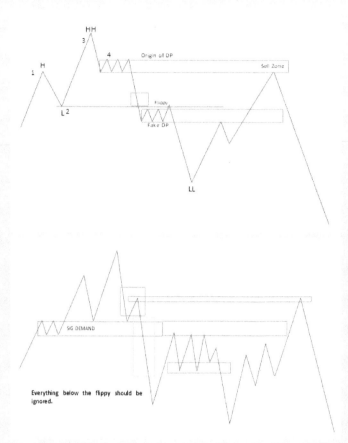

Everything below the flippy should be
ignored.

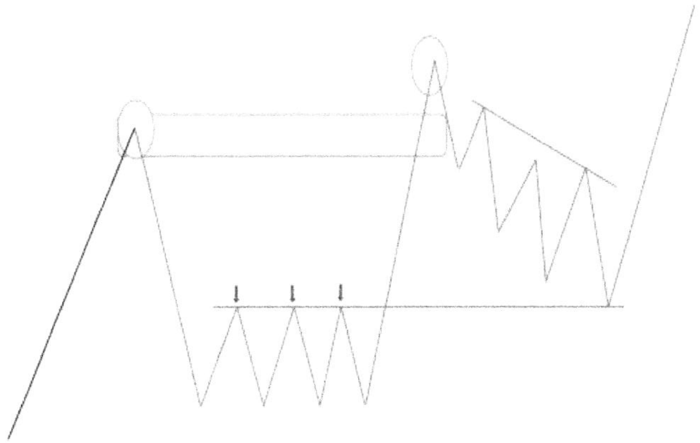

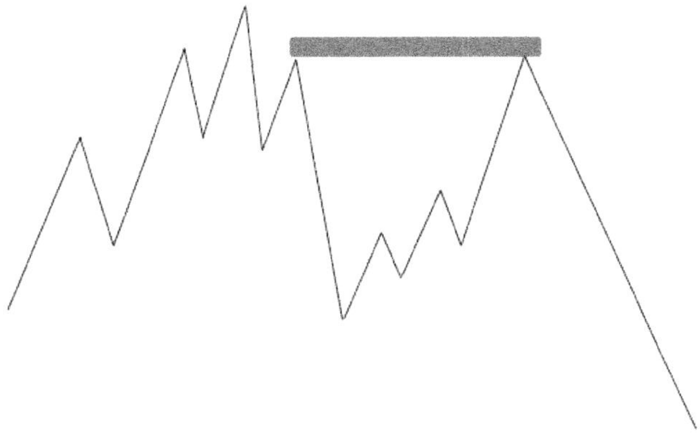

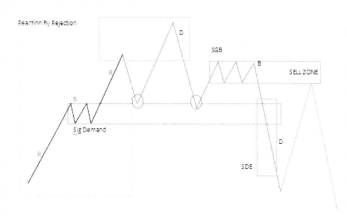

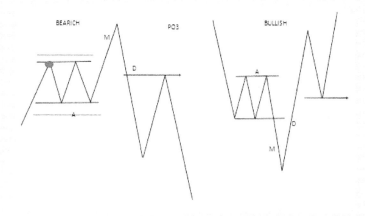

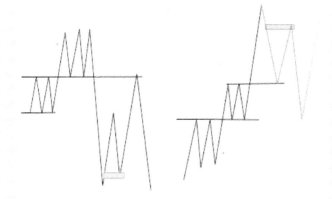

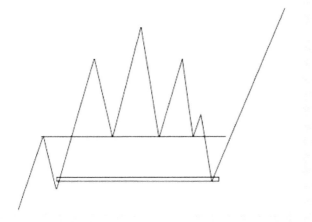

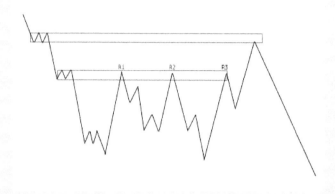

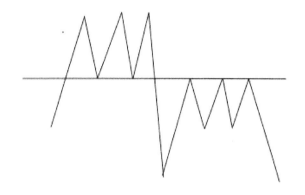

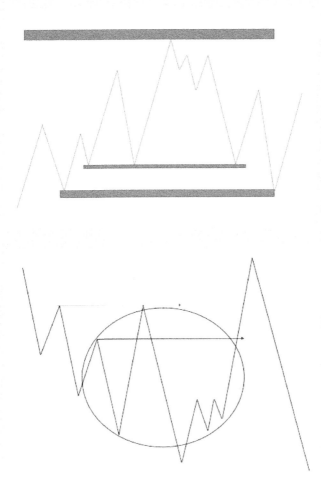

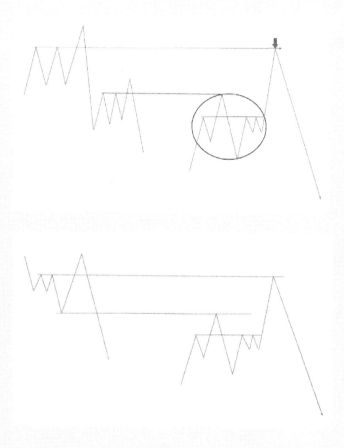

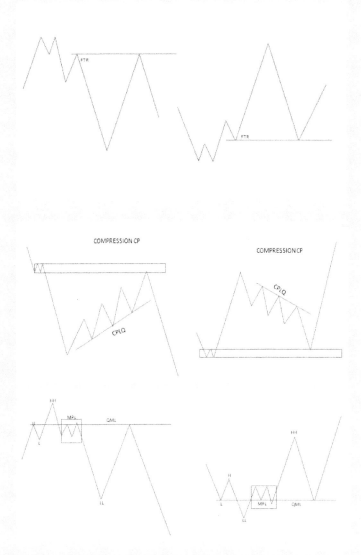

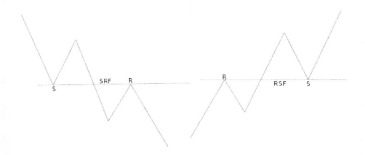

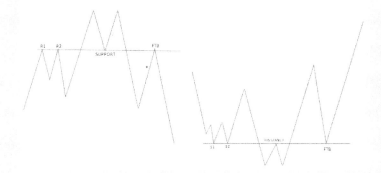

PREMIUM QML (FOZ, CPLQ).

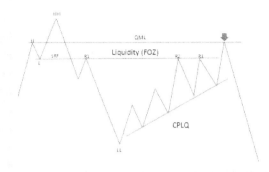

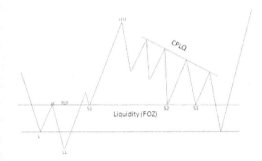

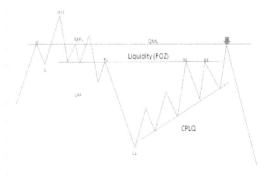

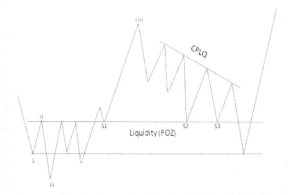

I believe that if you want to become a really good forex trader, having a solid understanding of order flow trading is crucial. Order flow trading simply provides you with that extra level of understanding that enables you to have a much better understanding of what's actually happening in the market and why various events are taking place. Price action trading and other types of trading can only take you so far.

Made in the USA
Las Vegas, NV
17 November 2024

11970970R00059